Mastering The Art Of Mindful Thinking

Mastering The Art Of Mindful Thinking
Copyright © 2023
Rob Taylor Books Publishing
Rob Taylor Author

Cover Art by robtaylorbooks.com
Cover Copyright ©Rob Taylor Books Publishing
Rob Taylor Author

Rob Taylor Books Publishing and Rob Taylor Author supports the right to free expression and the value of copyright. The purpose of copyright is to encourage writers and artists to produce creative works that enrich our culture.

Unauthorized distribution of this book is a violation of the author's intellectual property. If you would like permission to use material from this book (other than for review purposes), please contact Rob Taylor Books Publishing
robtaylorbooks.com
Thank you for respecting the author's rights.

Ebook ISBN: 978-1-0698264-6-6
Paperback ISBN: 978-1-0698264-2-8
Hardcover ISBN: 978-1-0698264-5-9

All rights reserved. No part of this publication may be reproduced without the prior written permission of both the copyright owner and the publisher of this book. © Copyright Rob Taylor 2023

Mastering the Art of Mindful Thinking

By Rob Taylor

Course Description

Welcome to "Mastering the Art of Mindful Thinking," a self-help course designed to help you overcome overthinking and regain control of your thoughts. In this course, we will explore the unique skill of stopping overthinking and tap into the power you already possess.

Through practical exercises and techniques, you will learn to clear your mind of baseless thoughts and replace them with factual and reality-based thinking patterns. By the end of this course, you will have the tools to redirect your focus, enhance your mental well-being, and cultivate a more grounded and purposeful mindset.

Course Outline

Module 1: Understanding Overthinking**

- Introduction to overthinking and its impact on mental well-being
- Recognizing the patterns of overthinking in your own life
- Identifying the negative consequences of excessive rumination

Module 2: The Power of Mindful Awareness

- Cultivating mindfulness as a foundation for mindful thinking
- Developing self-awareness to recognize when overthinking occurs

- Harnessing the present moment to anchor your thoughts

Module 3: Clearing Baseless Thoughts

- Distinguishing between thoughts based on reality and those rooted in fiction
- Identifying irrational and unfounded beliefs
- Techniques to challenge and debunk baseless thoughts

Module 4: Filling Your Thoughts with Facts

- Understanding the importance of factual thinking
- Differentiating between facts, predictions, and hypothetical scenarios

- Techniques to gather and analyze relevant information

Module 5: Redirecting Focus to the Present

- Shifting your attention from the future or past to the present moment
- Practicing mindfulness exercises to stay grounded in reality
- Cultivating gratitude and appreciation for the present moment

Module 6: Creating a Reality-Based Mindset

- Developing a realistic perspective on situations and events
- Overcoming cognitive biases and distorted thinking patterns

- Building resilience and adaptability through reality-based thinking

Module 7: Sustaining Mindful Thinking

- Developing a daily mindfulness practice
- Overcoming setbacks and challenges in maintaining mindful thinking
- Integrating mindful thinking into various aspects of your life

By the end of this course, you will have acquired the skills to break free from the cycle of overthinking and create a more reality-based and mindful thinking pattern. Get ready to embrace a more peaceful and grounded mindset as you embark on this transformative journey of self-discovery and personal growth.

Note: This course serves as a guide and provides general techniques for managing overthinking. If you are experiencing severe anxiety or mental health issues, it is recommended to seek professional help.

*** **Module 1** is an overview of what overthinking is and examples of physical and mental conditions that may occur from obsessive overthinking.*

*If you are familiar with these examples you can skip to **Module 2.***

Module 1 Understanding Overthinking

Introduction to overthinking and its impact on mental well-being

In our fast-paced and interconnected world, our minds are constantly bombarded with an overwhelming amount of information and stimuli. As a result, it's no surprise that many of us find ourselves caught in the web of overthinking. Overthinking refers to the incessant and repetitive process of dwelling on thoughts and analyzing situations from every possible angle. While introspection and reflection are vital for personal growth, overthinking can quickly spiral out of control and have a profound impact on our mental well-being.

Overthinking tends to manifest as a constant loop of rumination, where individuals find themselves trapped in a cycle of repetitive thoughts, worries, and self-doubt. These thoughts often revolve around past events, anticipating future scenarios, or excessively analyzing the present. What starts as a simple concern or a genuine desire to find solutions can quickly evolve into a never-ending mental treadmill.

The impact of overthinking on our mental well-being is far-reaching and multifaceted. First and foremost, overthinking heightens stress levels, as the mind becomes consumed by negative thought patterns and worst-case scenarios. This prolonged state of stress can lead to various physical and psychological health issues, including anxiety disorders, depression, insomnia, and even weakened immune system functioning.

Furthermore, overthinking can erode our ability to make decisions effectively. As we endlessly analyze and second-guess ourselves, the fear of making mistakes or choosing the wrong path can paralyze us, leaving us stuck in a state of indecision. This indecisiveness not only hinders our personal growth but also robs us of the opportunities and experiences that life presents.

Additionally, overthinking negatively impacts our relationships. When we are constantly preoccupied with our own thoughts and concerns, we may struggle to be fully present and engaged in our interactions with others. Over-thinkers often find themselves overanalyzing conversations, scrutinizing every word, and searching for hidden meanings that may not even exist. This hyper-vigilance can create unnecessary tension, miscommunication, and even strain relationships with loved ones.

In light of these detrimental effects, it becomes essential to understand the underlying causes of overthinking and explore strategies to break free from its grip. By fostering self-awareness, developing healthy coping mechanisms, and practicing mindfulness, individuals can reclaim control over their thoughts and cultivate a more balanced mental state.

In the following discussion, we will delve deeper into the causes and consequences of overthinking, examining its impact on mental well-being from various angles. We will also explore effective strategies and techniques to overcome overthinking, enabling individuals to regain clarity, peace of mind, and a more fulfilling life. Remember, breaking free from the chains of overthinking is not only possible but crucial for nurturing our mental well-being in today's complex world.

Recognizing the patterns of overthinking in your own life

Recognizing the patterns of overthinking in your own life can be a valuable step towards managing and overcoming this common cognitive tendency. Overthinking refers to the process of excessively analyzing, dwelling on, and ruminating over situations, events, or thoughts. It often leads to a heightened state of stress, anxiety, and indecision, hindering your ability to make clear and productive choices. Here are some detailed steps to help you recognize the patterns of overthinking in your own life:

• *Reflect on your thoughts and feelings*: Begin by creating a space for self-reflection. Pay attention to your thoughts and emotions throughout the day. Notice any recurring patterns or themes that tend to trigger overthinking. This could be related to specific areas of your life, such as work, relationships, or personal goals.

• ***Identify common triggers***: Once you have reflected on your thoughts and feelings, try to identify the common triggers that set off overthinking episodes. These triggers could be certain types of situations, interactions, or even specific thought patterns. For example, you may find that social interactions or upcoming deadlines tend to provoke overthinking in your life.

• ***Notice the physical and emotional signs***: Overthinking often manifests in physical and emotional symptoms. Pay attention to any signs that indicate you are entering an overthinking state. These may include increased heart rate, tense muscles, difficulty sleeping, irritability, or a sense of mental exhaustion. By recognizing these signs, you can become more aware of when overthinking is occurring.

• *Analyze the content and context of your thoughts*: Dive deeper into the content and context of your overthinking patterns. What are the specific thoughts that dominate your mind during these episodes? Are they related to past events, future scenarios, self-doubt, or perfectionism? Understanding the content of your thoughts can provide insights into the underlying beliefs and fears that fuel overthinking.

• *Track your thinking patterns*: Consider keeping a journal or using a note-taking app to track your thinking patterns throughout the day. When you notice an overthinking episode, write down the triggering event, your thoughts and emotions, and any resulting behaviours or decisions. This record can help you identify recurring patterns and gain a better understanding of your overthinking tendencies.

• *Seek external feedback*: Sometimes, it can be challenging to recognize our own overthinking patterns objectively. Reach out to trusted friends, family members, or a therapist to gain an outside perspective. Share your observations and experiences with them and ask for their insights. They may be able to provide valuable feedback and help you identify patterns that you may have missed.

- ***Challenge your thoughts and practice mindfulness***: Once you have identified your overthinking patterns, work on challenging the validity of your thoughts. Ask yourself if your thoughts are based on evidence or if they are distorted by anxiety or self-doubt. Practice mindfulness techniques to bring yourself into the present moment and shift your focus away from repetitive, unproductive thoughts.

- ***Develop coping strategies***: Lastly, develop and implement coping strategies to manage overthinking when it arises. This could involve engaging in relaxation exercises, such as deep breathing or meditation, setting aside dedicated "worry time" to address your concerns, or redirecting your attention to meaningful activities or hobbies. Experiment with different strategies to find what works best for you.

Remember that recognizing and addressing overthinking patterns is a gradual process. Be patient and compassionate with yourself as you navigate this journey towards greater self-awareness and healthier thinking habits.

Identifying the negative consequences of excessive rumination

Excessive rumination refers to the repetitive and persistent focus on negative thoughts, events, or emotions, often accompanied by over-analyzing and overthinking. While reflection and introspection can be healthy, excessive rumination can have several negative consequences on an individual's mental and emotional well-being. Here are some of the identified negative consequences of excessive rumination:

• *Increased Anxiety and Stress*: Excessive rumination tends to magnify and prolong feelings of anxiety and stress. Constantly replaying negative events or worries in the mind can heighten the physiological response associated with stress, such as increased heart rate, elevated cortisol levels, and muscle tension. This prolonged activation of the stress response can contribute to chronic anxiety and heightened emotional distress.

• *Depressive Symptoms*: Excessive rumination is strongly linked to the development and maintenance of depressive symptoms. Ruminating on negative experiences, past failures, or regrets can reinforce negative self-perceptions, decrease self-esteem, and amplify feelings of hopelessness and sadness. This negative cognitive pattern can contribute to the onset or exacerbation of depression.

• *Impaired Problem-Solving*: Excessive rumination tends to focus on the problem itself rather than exploring potential solutions. This narrow cognitive perspective limits creativity and flexibility in problem-solving. The repetitive nature of rumination often leads to a loop of negative thoughts and prevents individuals from finding effective solutions or taking appropriate action to address their concerns.

• *Interpersonal Difficulties*: Constantly dwelling on negative experiences or conflicts can strain interpersonal relationships. Excessive rumination can make individuals more self-focused, increasing their sensitivity to perceived slights or criticisms from others. This heightened self-consciousness can hinder effective communication, compromise empathy, and strain relationships with family, friends, or colleagues.

- *Sleep Disturbances*: Rumination often intensifies during nighttime when there are fewer distractions, leading to difficulties in falling asleep or maintaining a restful sleep. Intrusive negative thoughts can disrupt the sleep-wake cycle, causing insomnia or poor sleep quality. In turn, sleep disturbances can exacerbate existing mental health issues and impair overall cognitive functioning.

- *Reduced Cognitive Performance*: Excessive rumination consumes mental energy and attention, leaving less capacity for other cognitive processes. It can impair concentration, memory retrieval, and decision-making abilities. The constant preoccupation with negative thoughts and emotions can make it challenging to focus on tasks, leading to decreased productivity and performance in various areas of life.

- ***Physical Health Issues***: Prolonged periods of rumination can have detrimental effects on physical health. Chronic stress and anxiety associated with excessive rumination have been linked to increased risk of cardiovascular problems, weakened immune function, and heightened susceptibility to other stress-related disorders, such as headaches, gastrointestinal issues, and muscle pain.

It is important to note that excessive rumination is not a helpful coping strategy and does not lead to effective problem-solving or emotional resolution. If you or someone you know is struggling with excessive rumination, it is recommended to seek support from mental health professionals who can provide guidance and strategies to break free from this negative cognitive pattern.

Module 2: The Power of Mindful Awareness

Cultivating mindfulness as a foundation for mindful thinking

Cultivating mindfulness as a foundation for mindful thinking involves developing a deliberate and non-judgmental awareness of the present moment. It is the practice of paying attention to one's thoughts, emotions, and physical sensations without getting carried away by them or reacting impulsively. This state of mindfulness serves as a solid foundation for cultivating mindful thinking, which is characterized by clarity, objectivity, and wise decision-making. Let's explore this process in detail:

- ***Understanding Mindfulness***: Mindfulness is the ability to be fully present and engaged in the current moment. It involves observing thoughts, emotions, and sensations as they arise without attaching judgments or getting caught up in them. By developing this skill, individuals can cultivate a greater sense of self-awareness and an increased capacity to respond consciously to various situations.

- ***Practicing Mindfulness Meditation***: Mindfulness meditation is a powerful technique used to cultivate mindfulness. It involves setting aside dedicated time to focus attention on the breath, bodily sensations, or any anchor point chosen by the practitioner. Through regular practice, individuals become more adept at observing their thoughts and emotions without becoming entangled in them.

- ***Developing Non-judgmental Awareness***: Mindful thinking requires non-judgmental awareness, which means observing thoughts and experiences without labeling them as good or bad. This practice helps individuals detach from automatic patterns of judgment and encourages a more open and accepting attitude towards their own mental processes.

- ***Embracing the Present Moment***: Mindful thinking is rooted in the present moment. By bringing one's attention to the here and now, individuals can avoid ruminating about the past or worrying about the future. This focus on the present allows for a clearer perception of reality and helps reduce stress and anxiety.

• ***Cultivating Curiosity and Openness***: Mindful thinking encourages a curious and open mindset. Rather than clinging to preconceived notions or assumptions, individuals approach situations with a sense of wonder and a willingness to explore different perspectives. This open-mindedness promotes creativity, innovation, and the ability to consider alternative solutions.

• ***Developing Emotional Regulation***: Mindful thinking involves recognizing and regulating emotions effectively. By cultivating mindfulness, individuals develop the ability to observe their emotions without being overwhelmed by them. This heightened emotional intelligence allows for a more balanced and rational approach to decision-making.

• *Enhancing Cognitive Flexibility*: Mindful thinking expands cognitive flexibility, enabling individuals to break free from rigid thinking patterns. By observing thoughts objectively and recognizing cognitive biases, individuals can challenge their own assumptions and consider alternative viewpoints. This flexibility promotes adaptability and facilitates more informed and nuanced decision-making.

• *Applying Mindfulness in Daily Life*: The ultimate goal of cultivating mindfulness as a foundation for mindful thinking is to integrate it into everyday life. This means bringing a mindful awareness to all activities, whether it's eating, walking, working, or engaging in conversations. By practicing mindfulness in daily life, individuals can develop a sustained state of mindful thinking that permeates their thoughts, actions, and interactions with others.

In summary, cultivating mindfulness as a foundation for mindful thinking involves developing present-moment awareness, non-judgmental observation, and emotional regulation. It promotes curiosity, openness, and cognitive flexibility, allowing individuals to approach situations with clarity and wisdom. By integrating mindfulness into daily life, individuals can cultivate a sustained state of mindful thinking and experience numerous benefits, including improved well-being, enhanced decision-making, and better relationships with oneself and others.

Developing self-awareness to recognize when overthinking occurs

Developing self-awareness to recognize when overthinking occurs is an important skill that can greatly enhance one's mental well-being and overall quality of life. Overthinking refers to the tendency to excessively dwell on negative thoughts, worry excessively about the future, or endlessly analyze past events. It can lead to increased stress, anxiety, and a reduced ability to make decisions. By becoming more self-aware of the patterns and triggers associated with overthinking, individuals can take proactive steps to manage and redirect their thoughts. Here's a detailed guide on how to develop self-awareness and recognize when overthinking occurs:

- ***Educate yourself about overthinking***: Begin by understanding what overthinking is and how it affects your mental state. Read books, articles, or research studies on the subject to gain insights into the causes, symptoms, and consequences of overthinking. This knowledge will help you recognize the signs and patterns when they arise.

- ***Reflect on past experiences***: Take some time to reflect on your past experiences and try to identify instances when overthinking might have occurred. Consider situations where you felt overwhelmed by your thoughts, couldn't stop ruminating, or experienced excessive worry. Pay attention to any common themes, triggers, or thought patterns that tend to emerge during those moments.

- ***Observe your thoughts and emotions***: Throughout your day, make a conscious effort to observe your thoughts and emotions without judgment. Practice mindfulness techniques such as meditation or deep breathing exercises to cultivate a state of present-moment awareness. This practice will help you notice when your mind starts to wander into overthinking territory.

- ***Notice physical and emotional cues***: Overthinking often comes with physical and emotional cues that can act as warning signs. Pay attention to how your body feels when you're overthinking. It may manifest as tension in your muscles, increased heart rate, shallow breathing, or an overall feeling of unease. Additionally, observe your emotions. Are you feeling anxious, stressed, or overwhelmed? Recognizing these cues will help you identify when overthinking is taking hold.

• *Track your thoughts*: Keep a journal or use a note-taking app to jot down your thoughts whenever you catch yourself overthinking. Write down the specific situation, the thoughts running through your mind, and any associated emotions. This practice will create a record that allows you to identify recurring thought patterns and triggers.

• *Challenge your thoughts*: Once you've recognized that you're overthinking, challenge your thoughts by questioning their validity and exploring alternative perspectives. Ask yourself if there is evidence supporting your thoughts or if they are based on assumptions or irrational fears. Challenge negative self-talk and replace it with more balanced and realistic thinking.

• ***Engage in positive distractions***: When you notice overthinking taking hold, engage in activities that divert your attention and shift your focus away from the negative thoughts. Find hobbies, exercise, spend time with loved ones, or immerse yourself in activities that bring you joy. The goal is to break the cycle of rumination and redirect your energy towards more positive and productive endeavours.

• ***Seek support***: Don't hesitate to seek support from friends, family, or professionals if you're finding it challenging to manage your overthinking tendencies. Share your experiences and concerns with trusted individuals who can provide guidance, empathy, and a fresh perspective. Therapists or counsellors specializing in cognitive-behavioural therapy (CBT) can also offer effective strategies for managing overthinking.

• *Practice self-care*: Prioritize self-care activities that promote relaxation, stress reduction, and overall well-being. Engage in regular exercise, get sufficient sleep, maintain a balanced diet, and practice relaxation techniques such as deep breathing, yoga, or mindfulness meditation. Taking care of your physical and mental health can contribute to a clearer and more focused mind, making it easier to recognize and manage overthinking.

• *Maintain a growth mindset*: Embrace a growth mindset that acknowledges that overthinking is a habit that can be changed with practice and effort. Be patient with yourself and celebrate small victories along the way. Remember that developing self-awareness and managing overthinking is a journey, and with consistent effort, you can make significant progress.

By following these steps and remaining consistent in your efforts, you can develop self-awareness to recognize when overthinking occurs. This awareness will empower you to take control of your thoughts, redirect your focus, and cultivate a more balanced and peaceful state of mind.

Harnessing the present moment to anchor your thoughts

Harnessing the present moment to anchor your thoughts is a powerful practice that can help you cultivate mindfulness, enhance focus, and bring clarity to your thinking. By consciously directing your attention to the present moment, you can train your mind to stay grounded and centered, rather than being carried away by distractions or caught up in worries about the past or future. Here's a detailed explanation of how to harness the present moment to anchor your thoughts:

• *Set an intention*: Begin by setting an intention to anchor your thoughts in the present moment. This intention serves as a reminder and commitment to yourself to stay present and engaged with your current experience.

- *Create a conducive environment*: Find a quiet and comfortable space where you can minimize external distractions. This could be a peaceful room, a tranquil outdoor setting, or any place where you feel calm and relaxed.

- *Adopt a comfortable posture*: Choose a posture that allows you to be both alert and at ease. This could be sitting cross-legged on a cushion, sitting on a chair with your feet planted firmly on the ground, or even lying down if you can remain awake and attentive.

- *Focus on your breath*: Direct your attention to the sensation of your breath. Notice the inhales and exhales as they naturally occur. Feel the air entering and leaving your body, the rise and fall of your abdomen or chest, or any other physical sensations associated with breathing.

• ***Notice bodily sensations***: Expand your awareness to the physical sensations present in your body. Observe any tension, relaxation, warmth, coolness, or any other bodily sensations without judgment or the need to change them. Simply acknowledge their presence.

• ***Scan your surroundings***: Take a moment to observe and connect with your immediate environment. Notice the colours, shapes, and textures around you. Listen to the sounds in your environment, whether they are distant or nearby. Engage your senses fully to anchor yourself in the present moment.

• *Label your thoughts*: As thoughts arise, acknowledge them without getting entangled in them. You can mentally label your thoughts as "thinking" or "planning" to create some distance and objectivity. Allow the thoughts to come and go, like passing clouds in the sky, without attaching yourself to them.

• *Return to the present moment*: Whenever you find your thoughts wandering or getting caught up in the past or future, gently guide your attention back to the present moment. Use your breath or bodily sensations as an anchor to re-center your focus.

• *Practice non-judgmental awareness*: Cultivate a non-judgmental attitude toward your thoughts and experiences. Instead of labeling thoughts as good or bad, right or wrong, simply observe them with curiosity and acceptance. This helps you maintain an open and compassionate mindset.

• *Maintain consistency*: Consistency is key to reaping the benefits of this practice. Set aside regular periods throughout your day for anchoring your thoughts in the present moment. It could be a few minutes in the morning, during lunch breaks, or before bed. As you continue to practice, you'll find it easier to harness the present moment and anchor your thoughts throughout your daily life.

By consciously harnessing the present moment to anchor your thoughts, you develop the ability to stay focused, cultivate a clear mind, and cultivate a greater sense of peace and well-being in your life. This practice can be particularly helpful during times of stress, uncertainty, or when you need to make important decisions. With patience and persistence, you'll find that your ability to remain present and attentive deepens, leading to a more meaningful and fulfilling experience of life.

Module 3: Clearing Baseless Thoughts

Distinguishing between thoughts based on reality and those rooted in fiction

Distinguishing between thoughts based on reality and those rooted in fiction is a crucial cognitive process that helps us navigate the world and make informed decisions. Here, we'll delve into the details and explain the key characteristics that can help us differentiate between these two types of thoughts.

• *Source of Information*: Thoughts based on reality are typically derived from concrete and verifiable information obtained through personal experience, observation, or reliable sources. These thoughts align with objective facts, evidence, and logical reasoning. For example, if you remember having breakfast this morning or recall a conversation you had with a friend, those thoughts are likely based on reality.

In contrast, thoughts rooted in fiction originate from imagination, storytelling, creative thinking, or speculative scenarios. They may lack direct evidence or factual basis and often emerge from subjective interpretation or fictional narratives. If you find yourself daydreaming about flying on a dragon or envisioning a fantastical world, these thoughts are rooted in fiction.

• ***Consistency with External Reality***: Thoughts based on reality tend to be consistent with the external world and can be confirmed or corroborated by others. They are grounded in objective truths that can be tested or validated. For instance, if you think about the colour of the sky being blue or the sun rising in the east, these thoughts align with our shared reality.

On the other hand, thoughts rooted in fiction may deviate from external reality and reflect imaginative elements or fantastical constructs. They may include imaginary characters, places, events, or phenomena that do not exist or differ significantly from the known reality. If you envision a world where gravity works differently or where mythical creatures roam, these thoughts are likely rooted in fiction.

- *Evidence and Logical Coherence*: Thoughts based on reality are supported by evidence and follow a logical and coherent train of thought. They are grounded in cause-and-effect relationships, empirical data, and logical consistency. For example, if you analyze scientific research or engage in deductive reasoning based on available evidence, your thoughts are rooted in reality.

Conversely, thoughts rooted in fiction may lack direct evidence or logical coherence. They can freely transcend the boundaries of reality and incorporate elements that defy our known laws or principles. These thoughts often rely on imagination, symbolism, metaphor, or allegory to create narrative arcs or explore imaginative scenarios. When you imagine yourself as a superhero or envision a magical realm, these thoughts are based on fiction.

- *Emotional Response*: Our emotional response can also serve as a clue to distinguish between thoughts based on reality and those rooted in fiction. Thoughts rooted in reality often evoke emotions that correspond to the situation at hand. If you recall a happy memory and experience a sense of joy or reminisce about a sad event and feel melancholy, these emotions reflect the reality of your thoughts. In contrast, thoughts rooted in fiction can evoke emotions associated with imaginative or hypothetical scenarios. If you feel excitement, awe, or fear while daydreaming about encountering extraterrestrial life or exploring a haunted mansion, these emotions are likely tied to your fictional thoughts.

It's important to note that thoughts based on reality and those rooted in fiction are not mutually exclusive. Our minds have the capacity to integrate both aspects and imagine possibilities beyond the immediate reality. This ability allows us to engage in creative thinking, problem-solving, and speculative reasoning while still maintaining a connection to the real world.

Identifying irrational and unfounded beliefs

Identifying irrational and unfounded beliefs is an important skill for critical thinking and personal growth. These beliefs are often based on flawed reasoning, lack of evidence, or emotional biases. Here's a step-by-step process to help you identify and understand irrational and unfounded beliefs:

   • *Self-reflection*: Begin by reflecting on your own beliefs and examining them objectively. Consider areas of your life where you may hold strong opinions or assumptions without substantial evidence or logical reasoning. It could be beliefs related to politics, religion, relationships, personal abilities, or any other topic.

- *Questioning assumptions*: Challenge your own assumptions by asking critical questions. For example, ask yourself why you hold a particular belief, what evidence supports it, and whether it aligns with objective facts or logical reasoning. Consider alternative perspectives and try to see the issue from different angles.

- *Examining emotional biases*: Emotions can often cloud our judgment and lead to irrational beliefs. Identify any emotional biases that might influence your beliefs, such as fear, wishful thinking, or past experiences. Emotional biases can blind us to logical inconsistencies or contradictory evidence.

- *Seeking evidence*: Look for objective evidence and reliable sources to support or challenge your beliefs.

Evaluate the quality of the evidence by considering its source, credibility, and whether it's backed by scientific research or reputable studies. Avoid relying solely on anecdotal evidence or confirmation bias (the tendency to seek out information that confirms our preexisting beliefs).

• *Analyzing logical fallacies*: Familiarize yourself with common logical fallacies that can lead to irrational beliefs. Logical fallacies are errors in reasoning that can make an argument or belief appear valid when it is not. Some common fallacies include ad hominem attacks (attacking the person instead of their argument), appeals to authority, or circular reasoning.

• *Testing beliefs against reality*: Examine how well your beliefs align with objective reality and empirical evidence. Are there any real-world observations or experiences that contradict your beliefs? Consider conducting experiments or seeking out experiences that can provide a more accurate understanding of the subject matter.

• *Seeking diverse perspectives*: Engage in discussions and debates with people who hold different viewpoints. Exposing yourself to a variety of perspectives can challenge your existing beliefs and help you gain a more nuanced understanding of the subject. It's important to approach these conversations with an open mind and a willingness to consider alternative viewpoints.

• *Continual reassessment*: Recognize that beliefs are not set in stone and can evolve over time. Stay open to new evidence and be willing to revise or abandon beliefs that are proven to be irrational or unfounded. Regularly reassess your beliefs and be aware of cognitive biases that might hinder your ability to objectively evaluate new information.

By following these steps, you can develop a more rational and evidence-based mindset, free from irrational and unfounded beliefs. Remember, critical thinking and self-reflection are ongoing processes, and it's important to continually challenge and evaluate your beliefs to promote personal growth and intellectual development.

Techniques to challenge and debunk baseless thoughts

When faced with baseless thoughts, it's important to challenge and debunk them in order to foster critical thinking and maintain a rational perspective. Here are several techniques you can employ to effectively address and debunk baseless thoughts:

- *Critical questioning*: Ask yourself critical questions to examine the foundation of the baseless thought. Consider the evidence, logic, and reasoning behind it. For example:

  - What evidence supports this thought?
  - Are there any logical fallacies in the argument?
  - What assumptions underlie this thought?

- Are there any alternative explanations or perspectives?

- *Fact-checking*: Engage in thorough fact-checking to verify the accuracy of the claims made within the baseless thought. Look for reliable sources of information, consult experts, and cross-reference multiple sources to obtain an objective understanding of the topic.

- *Logical analysis*: Apply logical reasoning to evaluate the coherence of the baseless thought. Look for any inconsistencies or contradictions in the argument. Identify any faulty premises or flawed reasoning that may be present.

- *Skepticism and skepticism*: Approach the baseless thought with a healthy dose of skepticism. Maintain an open mind but require sufficient evidence to support any claims. Be cautious of confirmation bias, which can lead to accepting information that aligns with pre-existing beliefs while ignoring contradictory evidence.

- **Critical thinking tools**: Utilize critical thinking tools and frameworks to analyze the baseless thought. For example:

- *Occam's Razor*: Prefer the simplest explanation that accounts for the available evidence.
- *Logical fallacy identification*: Be familiar with common fallacies such as ad hominem attacks, false dichotomies, straw man arguments, etc.
- *Bayesian reasoning*: Evaluate the prior probability and update beliefs based on new evidence.

- ***Engage in constructive dialogue***: Discuss the baseless thought with others who may hold different perspectives. Engaging in thoughtful conversation can help identify flaws in the argument and expose biases. Be open to listening to counterarguments and adjusting your position accordingly.

- ***Empirical evidence***: Seek empirical evidence that supports or refutes the baseless thought. Rely on scientific studies, experiments, and peer-reviewed research. Analyze the quality of the evidence and the methodology used in conducting the studies.

- ***Seek expert opinions***: Consult subject matter experts or professionals in the relevant field to gain insights and expert opinions on the baseless thought. Experts can provide informed perspectives based on their knowledge and experience.

• ***Metacognition***: Reflect on your own cognitive biases and cognitive distortions that might influence your perception of the baseless thought. Be aware of factors such as emotional reasoning, availability bias, or the bandwagon effect that might cloud your judgment.

• ***Re-evaluate personal beliefs***: Be willing to modify or change your own beliefs when confronted with evidence that contradicts the baseless thought. Allow new information to reshape your understanding and promote intellectual growth.

Remember, debunking baseless thoughts requires patience, critical thinking skills, and a commitment to seeking truth and evidence-based reasoning. By employing these techniques, you can effectively challenge and debunk baseless thoughts and foster a more rational and informed perspective.

Module 4: Filling Your Thoughts with Facts

Understanding the importance of factual thinking

Introduction:

Factual thinking is a cognitive process that involves critically analyzing information, relying on evidence and facts to form accurate conclusions and make informed decisions. In today's era of information overload and the prevalence of misinformation, understanding the importance of factual thinking is crucial. This article will delve into the concept of factual thinking, highlight its significance in various aspects of life, and provide practical tips for cultivating this valuable skill.

I. *What is Factual Thinking?*

Factual thinking is the ability to evaluate information objectively and discern fact from opinion or falsehood. It involves employing critical thinking skills, logical reasoning, and a commitment to evidence-based analysis. Factual thinkers prioritize accuracy and seek reliable sources of information, employing skepticism and fact-checking to avoid falling prey to biases, misconceptions, or misleading narratives.

II. *The Significance of Factual Thinking:*

• ***Decision-Making***: Factual thinking enables individuals to make well-informed decisions by considering reliable evidence and relevant facts. It helps in avoiding impulsive choices driven by emotions, biases, or misinformation.

- ***Problem-Solving***: Factual thinking is essential for effective problem-solving. By gathering accurate information, identifying root causes, and evaluating potential solutions based on evidence, individuals can develop informed strategies to tackle complex problems.

- ***Media Literacy***: In an era of fake news and misinformation, factual thinking is crucial for media literacy. It allows individuals to critically evaluate news sources, verify information, and distinguish between credible journalism and unreliable sources, thereby fostering an informed and discerning approach to consuming media.

- *Scientific Inquiry*: Factual thinking forms the foundation of scientific inquiry. Scientists rely on factual thinking to conduct rigorous research, analyze data, and draw valid conclusions. Embracing factual thinking promotes a scientific mindset and fosters advancements in various fields.

- *Personal Growth*: Factual thinking plays a role in personal growth and self-awareness. By questioning assumptions, exploring different perspectives, and seeking accurate information, individuals can expand their knowledge, challenge biases, and develop a more nuanced understanding of the world.

III. *Cultivating Factual Thinking*:

• ***Develop Critical Thinking Skills***: Engage in activities that promote critical thinking, such as analyzing arguments, evaluating evidence, and recognizing logical fallacies. This helps build a foundation for factual thinking.

• ***Verify Sources***: Always verify the credibility and reliability of information sources. Cross-reference information from multiple sources and consult reputable publications, peer-reviewed research, or experts in the field to ensure accuracy.

• ***Fact-Check Information***: Fact-checking is crucial to combat misinformation. Utilize fact-checking websites and resources to verify claims and scrutinize viral stories or rumours before accepting them as truth.

• *Challenge Assumptions*: Cultivate a mindset of curiosity and skepticism. Question your own beliefs, challenge assumptions, and seek evidence to support or refute them. This practice fosters open-mindedness and intellectual growth.

• *Practice Media Literacy*: Develop media literacy skills by critically evaluating news sources, identifying biases, and differentiating between facts and opinions. Be aware of clickbait, sensationalism, and confirmation bias, and actively seek diverse perspectives.

• *Embrace Continuous Learning*: Stay curious and commit to lifelong learning. Engage with diverse subjects, explore different disciplines, and seek out reputable educational resources to broaden your knowledge base and enhance factual thinking.

Conclusion:

Factual thinking is a vital cognitive skill that empowers individuals to make informed decisions, navigate complex issues, and combat misinformation. By cultivating critical thinking, verifying sources, and embracing a fact-based approach to information, we can develop a more accurate understanding of the world, contribute to our personal growth, and promote a society rooted in rationality, evidence, and truth.

Differentiating between facts, predictions, and hypothetical scenarios

Let's dive into creating and explaining differentiating factors between facts, predictions, and hypothetical scenarios.

Facts:

Facts are statements that are based on objective reality and can be verified or proven to be true. They are generally accepted as accurate and are not subject to change. Facts are based on evidence, observations, or established information. Here are a few examples of facts:

- The Earth orbits around the Sun.

- Water boils at 100 degrees Celsius at sea level.
- The capital of France is Paris.

Predictions:

Predictions are statements about future events or outcomes that are based on available information, trends, patterns, or expert opinions. They are not certain and can be subject to change based on various factors. Predictions are educated guesses or forecasts. Here are a few examples of predictions:

- The stock market will experience a downturn next month.
- The global population will reach 10 billion by 2050.
- The next iPhone model will have a larger display and improved camera.

Hypothetical Scenarios:

Hypothetical scenarios are imagined situations or conditions that are not based on current reality. They are used to explore possibilities, hypothetical questions, or alternative outcomes. These scenarios are often used for discussions, debates, or creative purposes. Here are a few examples of hypothetical scenarios:

- What would happen if humans could teleport?
- If all cars were electric, how would it impact the environment?
- Suppose gravity stopped working for a day, what would occur?

The key differentiating factor between facts, predictions, and hypothetical scenarios lies in their basis and level of certainty.

- Facts are based on verifiable evidence or established information and are considered true. They describe the current state of affairs or past events.
- Predictions are statements about future events or outcomes based on available information, trends, or expert opinions. They are uncertain and can change based on new information.
- Hypothetical scenarios are imagined situations or conditions that explore possibilities or alternative outcomes. They are not based on reality and are used for creative or speculative purposes.

When evaluating information, it is essential to distinguish between these categories to understand the level of certainty and basis for each statement. Facts provide concrete and reliable information, predictions offer insights into possible future events, and hypothetical scenarios foster creative thinking and exploration of alternative possibilities.

Techniques to gather and analyze relevant information

Gathering and analyzing relevant information is crucial for decision-making, problem-solving, research, and many other activities. Here are some techniques you can use to gather and analyze information effectively:

• *Define your objective*: Clearly define your goal and the specific information you need to achieve it. This helps you focus your efforts and ensures you collect relevant data.

• *Primary and secondary research*: Primary research involves collecting data directly from original sources, such as surveys, interviews, experiments, or observations. Secondary research involves gathering data from existing sources like books, articles, reports, or databases. Utilize a combination of both to gather a comprehensive set of information.

• *Literature review*: Conduct a thorough literature review to gather existing knowledge and research on your topic. This helps you understand the current state of knowledge and identifies any research gaps or areas where further investigation is needed.

• *Surveys and questionnaires*: Design and administer surveys or questionnaires to collect data from a large number of people efficiently. Ensure your questions are clear, unbiased, and designed to gather the specific information you need.

• *Interviews*: Conduct interviews with experts or individuals who possess relevant knowledge or experience. Prepare a list of questions in advance, be an active listener, and ask follow-up questions to delve deeper into the subject matter.

• *Focus groups*: Organize focus groups consisting of a small number of people who share similar characteristics or experiences. Facilitate discussions among the participants to gather diverse perspectives and insights.

• *Data mining*: Utilize data mining techniques to extract useful information from large datasets. This involves applying algorithms to identify patterns, correlations, or trends within the data.

• *Content analysis*: Analyze written or verbal content, such as articles, speeches, social media posts, or customer feedback, to extract meaningful information. This technique helps identify common themes, sentiments, or key messages.

• ***Statistical analysis***: Apply statistical techniques to analyze numerical data and draw meaningful conclusions. This can involve calculating averages, correlations, regression analysis, or conducting hypothesis testing.

• ***Visualization techniques***: Use visual representations, such as charts, graphs, or diagrams, to summarize and present complex information. Visualizations help identify patterns or trends that may not be apparent in raw data.

• ***Comparative analysis***: Compare and contrast different sets of information to identify similarities, differences, or relationships. This technique helps gain insights into the factors that influence the outcomes you are examining.

• ***Critical thinking***: Apply critical thinking skills to evaluate the reliability, validity, and relevance of the gathered information. Look for biases, consider alternative perspectives, and question assumptions to ensure robust analysis.

• ***Synthesis***: Synthesize the gathered information by organizing it into meaningful categories or frameworks. This helps identify key findings, trends, or recommendations.

• ***Continuous learning***: Stay updated with the latest research, news, and developments related to your topic. Information is constantly evolving, and continuous learning ensures you have access to the most relevant and up-to-date information.

Remember, the choice of techniques may vary depending on the nature of your objective, available resources, and the specific domain or field you are working in. Flexibility and adaptability are key when gathering and analyzing information effectively.

Module 5: Redirecting Focus to the Present

Shifting your attention from the future or past to the present moment

Shifting your attention from the future or past to the present moment is an essential practice that can greatly enhance your overall well-being and quality of life. It involves consciously redirecting your thoughts, emotions, and focus away from thoughts of what has already happened or what may happen in the future, and instead, immersing yourself fully in the present moment. This practice is often referred to as mindfulness or present-moment awareness.

To shift your attention to the present moment, you can follow these steps:

- ***Recognize the need for presence***: Begin by acknowledging that your mind is either dwelling in the past or projecting into the future. Understand that by bringing your attention to the present, you can cultivate a greater sense of clarity, calmness, and engagement with your current experience.

- ***Ground yourself in the present***: Take a few deep breaths and use your senses to anchor yourself in the present moment. Notice the sensations in your body, the sounds around you, the temperature of the air, and any other sensory experiences that can help bring you into the present.

- ***Observe your thoughts and emotions***: As you become more present, you might notice that your mind continues to wander or gets caught up in thoughts and emotions. Instead of trying to push them away or get caught up in them, simply observe them without judgment. Acknowledge their presence and let them pass by, like clouds moving across the sky.

• *Engage with your surroundings*: Once you have established a sense of presence, engage fully with your immediate environment and the task at hand. Whether you're working, spending time with loved ones, or simply taking a walk, bring your full attention to the present moment. Notice the details, the nuances, and the richness of the experience.

• *Cultivate gratitude and appreciation*: Shift your focus to gratitude and appreciation for the present moment. Recognize the blessings, opportunities, and beauty that surround you right now. This helps foster a positive mindset and deepens your connection with the present.

• *Practice mindfulness in daily activities*: Extend this practice of presence into your daily activities. Whether it's eating, showering, exercising, or doing chores, approach each activity with mindfulness. Pay attention to the sensations, movements, and actions involved, fully immersing yourself in the present experience.

• *Reduced stress and anxiety*: By focusing on the present moment, you can alleviate stress and anxiety related to the past or future events. Mindfulness helps you break free from negative thought patterns and cultivates a sense of calmness and clarity.

• *Improved mental well-being*: Being fully present allows you to savour the joys and simple pleasures of life. It enhances your ability to experience happiness, contentment, and peace of mind, fostering overall mental well-being.

• *Enhanced productivity and focus*: When you direct your attention to the present moment, you can concentrate better on the task at hand. This heightened focus leads to increased productivity, efficiency, and effectiveness in your work and daily activities.

• *Deeper connections with others*: Mindful presence allows you to listen attentively, empathize, and connect more deeply with others. By being fully engaged in conversations and interactions, you build stronger relationships and promote meaningful connections.

• *Greater self-awareness and personal growth*: Shifting your attention to the present moment enhances self-awareness. It helps you observe your thoughts, emotions, and behaviours without judgment, enabling personal growth, self-reflection, and a deeper understanding of yourself.

Remember, shifting your attention to the present moment is a continuous practice that requires patience and persistence. By cultivating present-moment awareness, you can live a more fulfilling and meaningful life, grounded in the richness of the here and now.

Practicing mindfulness exercises to stay grounded in reality

Practicing mindfulness exercises can be a powerful tool to stay grounded in reality and enhance your overall well-being. Mindfulness is the practice of intentionally bringing your attention to the present moment without judgment. By focusing on the present, you can cultivate a deeper sense of awareness and develop a clearer understanding of reality as it unfolds. Here are some mindfulness exercises you can try to stay grounded:

• *Mindful Breathing*: Find a quiet and comfortable place to sit or lie down. Close your eyes and take a few deep breaths, allowing your body to relax. Begin to focus your attention on the sensation of your breath as it enters and leaves your body. Notice the rise and fall of your abdomen or the feeling of air passing through your nostrils. Whenever your mind wanders, gently guide your attention back to your breath. Practice this exercise for a few minutes or as long as you wish.

• *Body Scan*: Sit or lie down in a comfortable position and bring your awareness to your body. Starting from the top of your head, slowly scan your body from head to toe, paying attention to any sensations, tensions, or areas of relaxation that you notice. Allow yourself to fully experience each part of your body without judgment. This exercise helps you develop a deeper connection with your physical self and promotes a sense of grounding.

• ***Sensory Awareness***: Choose an object, such as a piece of fruit, a small trinket, or a flower. Take a few moments to observe it closely. Notice its colours, textures, and shapes. Engage your senses fully by exploring its scent, taste, and even the sound it might make when touched. This exercise helps anchor your attention in the present moment and encourages you to appreciate the richness of sensory experiences.

• ***Walking Meditation***: Find a quiet space where you can walk uninterrupted. Begin to walk at a slow and steady pace, focusing your attention on the physical sensations of walking. Pay attention to the movement of your feet, the shifting of your weight, and the sensation of the ground beneath you. Stay fully present as you walk, letting go of any thoughts or distractions that arise. Walking meditation allows you to integrate mindfulness into your daily activities and connect with your body and surroundings.

• *Mindful Observation*: Choose an everyday object, such as a pencil, a cup, or a leaf. Take a few minutes to observe it mindfully. Explore its details, textures, and colours. Engage your senses by noticing any sounds, smells, or even tastes associated with the object. Allow yourself to be fully present with the object, observing it as if for the first time. This exercise cultivates a sense of curiosity and helps you become more attuned to the intricacies of your immediate environment.

Remember, mindfulness is a skill that develops with regular practice. Start with short sessions and gradually increase the duration as you become more comfortable. The key is to approach these exercises with an open and non-judgmental attitude, accepting whatever thoughts, feelings, or sensations arise during the practice. By practicing mindfulness exercises regularly, you can strengthen your ability to stay grounded in reality and experience a greater sense of peace and clarity in your daily life.

Cultivating gratitude and appreciation for the present moment

Cultivating gratitude and appreciation for the present moment is a powerful practice that can enhance our overall well-being and bring us greater joy and contentment in life. It involves developing an awareness of the present moment and consciously recognizing and acknowledging the positive aspects of our current experiences. Here's a detailed explanation of how to cultivate gratitude and appreciation for the present moment:

• *Mindful Awareness*: Begin by cultivating mindful awareness, which involves being fully present and engaged in the current moment. Set aside distractions, such as electronic devices, and create a space of calm and stillness where you can focus on the present.

• ***Pause and Reflect***: Take a moment to pause and reflect on the present moment. Notice your surroundings, the sensations in your body, and the thoughts and emotions that arise. Allow yourself to fully experience the present without judgment or the need to change anything.

• ***Gratitude Journaling***: Keep a gratitude journal to record things you are grateful for in the present moment. Each day, write down three to five things that you appreciate or feel grateful for. They can be simple things like a beautiful sunrise, a kind gesture from a friend, or a delicious meal. This practice helps shift your focus to the positive aspects of your life.

- *Savour Experiences*: Practice savouring the present moment by fully immersing yourself in enjoyable experiences. Whether it's sipping a cup of tea, going for a walk in nature, or spending time with loved ones, pay attention to the details and relish the experience. Engage all your senses and appreciate the richness of the moment.

- *Gratitude Meditation*: Incorporate gratitude meditation into your daily routine. Find a comfortable position, close your eyes, and take a few deep breaths to center yourself. Bring to mind something you are grateful for in the present moment and hold it in your awareness. Allow feelings of gratitude and appreciation to arise and expand within you. You can also visualize sending gratitude and well-wishes to others.

• *Acts of Kindness*: Engage in acts of kindness and generosity toward others. By expressing gratitude and appreciation to others, you not only cultivate positive emotions within yourself but also strengthen your connections with those around you. Whether it's a small gesture or a significant action, acts of kindness help foster a sense of gratitude and compassion.

• *Acceptance and Letting Go*: Practice accepting the present moment as it is, without attachment to how things should be or regrets about the past. Acceptance allows you to embrace the present fully and appreciate its unique qualities. Let go of judgment and criticism, and cultivate an attitude of non-resistance.

• *Gratitude Reminders*: Use visual or auditory reminders throughout your day to prompt gratitude and appreciation. It could be placing a gratitude quote on your desk, setting a reminder on your phone, or wearing a piece of jewelry that holds a special meaning. These reminders serve as cues to bring your attention back to the present and encourage gratitude.

• *Gratitude in Challenging Times*: Recognize that cultivating gratitude and appreciation doesn't mean ignoring or denying the difficulties and challenges you may be facing. Instead, it involves finding moments of gratitude within those circumstances, such as the lessons learned, personal growth, or the support you receive from others.

By regularly practicing these steps, you can develop a habit of cultivating gratitude and appreciation for the present moment. Over time, this mindset shift can bring more joy, contentment, and resilience to your life, and help you find beauty and blessings in the ordinary moments that make up your daily existence

Module 6: Creating a Reality-Based Mindset

Developing a realistic perspective on situations and events

Developing a realistic perspective on situations and events is a valuable skill that involves examining things as they are, free from excessive bias, assumptions, or wishful thinking. It requires a thoughtful and objective approach to understanding the world around us. Here's a step-by-step guide to developing a realistic perspective:

• *Seek diverse sources of information*: To gain a realistic perspective, it's crucial to gather information from a variety of sources. Relying on a single source or a specific viewpoint can lead to a biased understanding of situations. Engage with different media outlets, read books from various authors, explore academic research, and engage in discussions with people who have diverse perspectives. This helps you obtain a broader range of viewpoints and avoid falling into an echo chamber.

• ***Practice critical thinking***: Critical thinking is the ability to evaluate information objectively and analyze it for reliability, credibility, and logical coherence. Develop critical thinking skills by questioning the information you encounter. Consider the source's credibility, check for supporting evidence, and assess the logical consistency of the arguments presented. This process helps you identify biases, logical fallacies, and weak arguments, enabling you to form a more realistic understanding.

•*Understand cognitive biases*: Cognitive biases are inherent flaws in human thinking that can distort our perception of reality. Familiarize yourself with common biases such as confirmation bias (tendency to favour information that confirms existing beliefs), availability bias (relying on readily available information), and anchoring bias (relying too heavily on initial information). By recognizing these biases, you can consciously challenge them and strive for a more objective viewpoint.

• *Consider multiple perspectives*: Realistic perspectives often involve considering different viewpoints on a given situation or event. Put yourself in the shoes of others and try to understand their motivations, values, and beliefs. This exercise helps you gain empathy and a broader understanding of complex issues. Recognize that different perspectives can coexist, and a nuanced understanding can emerge by considering multiple viewpoints.

• *Analyze evidence and facts*: A realistic perspective relies on evidence and facts rather than personal opinions or emotions. Develop a habit of fact-checking and verifying information before accepting it as true. Scrutinize the quality of evidence, cross-reference information from reliable sources, and consult experts in relevant fields when needed. This analytical approach helps you separate truth from misinformation or disinformation, contributing to a more realistic perspective.

- ***Embrace uncertainty***: Realistic perspectives acknowledge the inherent uncertainty of the world. Recognize that situations and events are often complex and multifaceted, and absolute certainty may be elusive. Embracing uncertainty allows you to avoid premature judgments or hasty conclusions, fostering a more realistic and open-minded outlook.

- ***Reflect and revise***: Regularly reflect on your perspectives and revisit them as new information emerges. Be open to adjusting your views based on new evidence or insights. Cultivating a growth mindset and a willingness to learn and adapt is essential for developing a realistic perspective over time.

Remember, developing a realistic perspective is an ongoing process. It requires continuous learning, self-reflection, and the willingness to challenge your own beliefs. By following these steps and maintaining an open mind, you can foster a more accurate understanding of the world around you.

Overcoming cognitive biases and distorted thinking patterns

Overcoming cognitive biases and distorted thinking patterns can be a challenging but rewarding endeavour. These biases and patterns are inherent to human thinking and can significantly influence our judgments and decision-making processes. However, by developing awareness and implementing specific strategies, we can effectively mitigate their impact. Here's a detailed explanation of how to overcome cognitive biases and distorted thinking patterns:

• ***Develop self-awareness***: The first step in overcoming cognitive biases and distorted thinking patterns is to cultivate self-awareness. Recognize that everyone is susceptible to biases, including yourself.

Acknowledge that these biases can cloud your judgment and affect your decision-making.

• *Learn about common biases*: Educate yourself about common cognitive biases and distorted thinking patterns. Familiarize yourself with concepts such as confirmation bias, availability heuristic, anchoring effect, and others. Understanding these biases will help you recognize them when they arise.

• *Challenge your assumptions*: Actively question your assumptions and beliefs. Be open to different perspectives and seek out information that challenges your existing views. This can help you overcome confirmation bias, which is the tendency to seek information that supports your preconceived notions while ignoring contradictory evidence.

• *Practice critical thinking*: Develop your critical thinking skills by evaluating information and arguments objectively. Assess the quality of evidence, question sources, and consider alternative explanations. Engaging in critical thinking can counteract biases like the availability heuristic, which leads us to rely on easily accessible information.

• *Slow down and reflect*: Take your time when making important decisions. Slow down and reflect on the information available to you. Avoid rushing to judgments based on initial impressions or emotional reactions. This can help you overcome biases like the primacy effect or the affect heuristic.

- *Utilize decision-making frameworks*: Implement decision-making frameworks that encourage systematic and rational thinking. For example, consider using the SWOT analysis (Strengths, Weaknesses, Opportunities, Threats) or cost-benefit analysis to evaluate options objectively. These frameworks can help counteract biases like the framing effect.

- *Embrace uncertainty*: Accept that uncertainty is a natural part of decision-making. Avoid the temptation to rely on absolute certainty or overconfidence. Embracing uncertainty can help you overcome biases such as the overconfidence effect and the illusion of control.

- ***Learn from past experiences***: Reflect on your past decisions and evaluate their outcomes. Analyze whether biases or distorted thinking patterns influenced your choices and identify areas for improvement. This practice of learning from experience can help you refine your decision-making process.

- *Seek feedback*: Actively seek feedback from others, especially those who may challenge your thinking. Embrace constructive criticism and be open to revising your viewpoints. Feedback can help you identify blind spots and correct cognitive biases.

- ***Practice mindfulness***: Engage in mindfulness practices that help you develop present-moment awareness and non-judgmental observation of your thoughts and emotions.

Mindfulness can enhance your ability to notice and disengage from biases, allowing for clearer and more objective thinking.

• *Continuously learn and adapt*: Overcoming cognitive biases and distorted thinking patterns is an ongoing process. Stay curious, remain open to new information, and continuously strive to improve your thinking skills. Embrace a growth mindset that acknowledges the potential for biases and actively seeks methods to overcome them.

By following these strategies and incorporating them into your daily life, you can effectively overcome cognitive biases and distorted thinking patterns. It may take time and effort, but the result will be more informed decisions, enhanced critical thinking, and a broader perspective on the world around you.

Building resilience and adaptability through reality-based thinking

Building resilience and adaptability through reality-based thinking is a process that involves developing a mindset and skills to effectively navigate and thrive in challenging situations. This approach emphasizes a realistic assessment of one's circumstances and the ability to adapt and respond appropriately. Here's a detailed explanation of the steps involved in building resilience and adaptability through reality-based thinking:

- *Embrace reality*: The first step in reality-based thinking is acknowledging and accepting the current situation as it is. This involves recognizing both the positive and negative aspects of the situation without denying or exaggerating them. By accepting reality, individuals can let go of wishful thinking or dwelling on the past, enabling them to focus on the present and future possibilities.

• *Cultivate self-awareness*: Developing self-awareness is crucial for reality-based thinking. It involves understanding one's strengths, weaknesses, emotions, and thought patterns. By being aware of their own beliefs, biases, and limitations, individuals can approach situations with a more objective perspective and make better-informed decisions.

• *Develop flexible thinking*: Resilience and adaptability require the ability to think flexibly and consider multiple perspectives. It's important to challenge rigid thinking patterns and explore alternative solutions or approaches. This involves questioning assumptions, seeking diverse opinions, and embracing uncertainty. By adopting a growth mindset and being open to new ideas, individuals can adapt more effectively to changing circumstances.

• *Practice problem-solving*: Reality-based thinking involves developing strong problem-solving skills. This includes breaking down complex problems into smaller, manageable parts, identifying potential obstacles and risks, and generating creative solutions. By focusing on realistic and practical strategies, individuals can enhance their ability to address challenges and find effective solutions.

- ***Develop emotional intelligence***: Emotional intelligence plays a significant role in building resilience and adaptability. It involves recognizing and managing emotions, both in oneself and others. By developing emotional resilience, individuals can effectively cope with stress, setbacks, and adversity. This includes practicing self-care, seeking support when needed, and maintaining a positive outlook.

- ***Learn from experiences***: Building resilience and adaptability requires learning from past experiences. It involves reflecting on successes and failures, identifying lessons learned, and applying those insights to future situations. By adopting a growth mindset and viewing challenges as opportunities for growth, individuals can build a reservoir of knowledge and skills that enhance their ability to adapt in the face of adversity.

• *Seek feedback*: Feedback is an essential component of reality-based thinking. Actively seeking feedback from trusted mentors, colleagues, or supervisors can provide valuable insights into blind spots and areas for improvement. By being open to feedback and incorporating it into personal development, individuals can continuously refine their thinking and decision-making processes.

• *Build a support network*: Having a strong support network is crucial for building resilience and adaptability. Surrounding oneself with positive and supportive individuals who share similar values and goals can provide encouragement, advice, and perspective during challenging times. It's important to foster and maintain these relationships, as they can contribute to emotional well-being and provide valuable support in times of change or uncertainty.

By incorporating these steps into one's mindset and daily practices, individuals can gradually develop resilience and adaptability through reality-based thinking. This approach allows them to navigate through setbacks, overcome obstacles, and embrace change with confidence and effectiveness.

Module 7: Sustaining Mindful Thinking

Developing a daily mindfulness practice

Developing a daily mindfulness practice can have numerous benefits for your mental, emotional, and physical well-being. Mindfulness is the practice of intentionally bringing your attention to the present moment, without judgment or attachment. It involves cultivating awareness of your thoughts, feelings, bodily sensations, and the environment around you. By incorporating mindfulness into your daily routine, you can reduce stress, enhance focus, improve emotional regulation, and foster a greater sense of overall contentment. Here's a step-by-step guide to developing a daily mindfulness practice:

- *Set an Intention*: Begin by setting a clear intention for your mindfulness practice. Ask yourself why you want to cultivate mindfulness and what you hope to gain from it. This intention will serve as your guiding principle throughout the process.

- *Choose a Time*: Determine the best time for your mindfulness practice. It could be in the morning, before starting your day, or in the evening, to unwind and relax. Select a time when you can dedicate at least 10-15 minutes without interruptions.

- *Find a Quiet Space*: Identify a quiet and comfortable space where you can practice mindfulness. It could be a specific room in your home, a cozy corner, or even a serene outdoor spot. Ensure that you won't be disturbed during your practice.

• *Adopt a Comfortable Posture*: Assume a comfortable posture that promotes alertness and relaxation. You can sit cross-legged on a cushion, in a chair with your feet flat on the ground, or even lie down if that's more suitable. Keep your spine straight and your body relaxed.

•*Focus on the Breath*: Start your mindfulness practice by bringing your attention to your breath. Notice the sensation of the breath as it enters and leaves your body. You can place your hand on your abdomen to feel the rising and falling with each breath. Allow your breath to be your anchor, bringing your attention back whenever it wanders.

- *Scan the Body*: After a few minutes of focusing on the breath, shift your attention to your body. Slowly scan through different parts of your body, from head to toe, noticing any sensations, tensions, or areas of relaxation. If you encounter any discomfort, simply observe it without judgment.

- *Cultivate Non-Judgmental Awareness*: As you continue your mindfulness practice, cultivate a non-judgmental attitude towards your thoughts, feelings, and bodily sensations. Instead of labeling experiences as good or bad, simply observe them as they arise and pass away. Notice any tendencies to cling or resist certain experiences and practice letting go.

- ***Engage the Senses***: Another way to cultivate mindfulness is by engaging your senses. Bring awareness to the sights, sounds, smells, tastes, and tactile sensations in your immediate environment. Fully immerse yourself in the present moment, savouring each experience as it unfolds.

- ***Practice Mindful Activities***: Extend mindfulness to your daily activities. Whether it's eating, walking, washing dishes, or brushing your teeth, bring your full attention to the task at hand. Notice the sensations, movements, and details involved in each activity, enhancing your overall awareness.

- ***Seek Guidance***: If you're new to mindfulness or desire additional support, consider seeking guidance from experienced teachers or joining a mindfulness group. Books, apps, and online resources can also provide valuable techniques and meditations to deepen your practice.

• ***Be Consistent and Gentle***: Establishing a daily mindfulness practice requires consistency and patience. Start with a realistic goal, such as practicing for 10 minutes a day, and gradually increase the duration as you become more comfortable. Be gentle with yourself and acknowledge that your mind will wander — this is normal. Whenever you notice your attention drifting, kindly bring it back to the present moment without self-criticism.

• ***Reflect and Integrate***: After each practice, take a moment to reflect on your experience. Notice any changes in your thoughts, emotions, or overall well-being. Consider how you can integrate mindfulness into your daily life beyond formal practice, bringing the benefits into your relationships, work, and self-care routines.

Remember, developing a daily mindfulness practice is a journey, and it may take time to fully experience the benefits. Embrace the process, stay committed, and approach each practice session with an open and curious mindset. With consistent effort, mindfulness can become a powerful tool for self-awareness and personal growth.

Overcoming setbacks and challenges in maintaining mindful thinking

Maintaining mindful thinking can be challenging, especially when faced with setbacks and obstacles. However, by employing certain strategies and adopting a resilient mindset, it is possible to overcome these challenges and continue on the path of mindful living. Here are some detailed steps and explanations on how to overcome setbacks and challenges in maintaining mindful thinking:

- *Recognize and accept setbacks*: The first step in overcoming setbacks is to acknowledge and accept their presence. It is normal to encounter challenges and obstacles along the way, and by recognizing them, you avoid denying or resisting their existence. Acceptance allows you to shift your mindset towards finding solutions rather than dwelling on the problem.

- *Cultivate self-compassion*: When setbacks occur, it's crucial to practice self-compassion. Treat yourself with kindness, understanding, and forgiveness. Recognize that setbacks are a part of life and that everyone experiences them. By being gentle with yourself, you can avoid self-judgment or negative self-talk that may hinder your ability to maintain mindful thinking.

- *Embrace imperfection*: Mindfulness is not about achieving perfection but rather about being present and accepting things as they are. Setbacks can create feelings of frustration or disappointment, but it's important to remind yourself that these moments do not define your mindfulness journey. Embracing imperfections allows you to let go of self-imposed expectations and remain focused on the present moment.

• ***Practice resilience***: Resilience is the ability to bounce back from setbacks and adapt to challenges. Cultivating resilience involves developing a growth mindset, where setbacks are viewed as opportunities for growth and learning. Instead of being discouraged by setbacks, see them as valuable lessons that can strengthen your mindfulness practice. Resilience enables you to persist and maintain mindful thinking even in the face of adversity.

• ***Reframe setbacks as learning experiences***: Rather than perceiving setbacks as failures, reframe them as learning experiences. Analyze the situation and identify what went wrong or what could be improved. By adopting a growth-oriented perspective, setbacks become valuable opportunities to refine your mindfulness practice and gain insight into yourself. Embrace setbacks as stepping stones towards personal growth and progress.

• *Seek support*: During challenging times, it can be beneficial to seek support from others. Engage with like-minded individuals, join mindfulness communities or groups, or seek guidance from a mindfulness teacher or therapist. Sharing your experiences and learning from others who have faced similar challenges can provide encouragement, validation, and new perspectives. Support from others can help you stay motivated and committed to maintaining mindful thinking.

• *Revisit your intentions and goals*: Setbacks can sometimes lead to a loss of focus or motivation. In such moments, revisit your intentions and goals for practicing mindfulness. Remind yourself of why you embarked on this journey in the first place and reconnect with your core values. Realigning with your purpose can reignite your passion for mindful living and help you overcome setbacks with renewed determination.

Remember that setbacks and challenges are a natural part of any transformative journey, including the practice of mindfulness. By approaching setbacks with resilience, self-compassion, and a growth mindset, you can navigate these obstacles and continue to cultivate and maintain mindful thinking in your life.

Integrating mindful thinking into various aspects of your life

Integrating mindful thinking into various aspects of your life can greatly enhance your overall well-being and improve the quality of your experiences. Mindful thinking involves being fully present in the moment, paying attention to your thoughts, feelings, and sensations without judgment. By cultivating a mindful mindset, you can develop a greater sense of self-awareness, manage stress effectively, and make conscious choices that align with your values. Here's how you can integrate mindful thinking into different areas of your life:

Mindful Thinking in Daily Routine:

• *Begin your day with a mindful ritual*: Instead of rushing through your morning routine, take a few moments to focus on your breath, set intentions for the day, and express gratitude.

• *Practice mindful eating*: Pay attention to the flavours, textures, and smells of your food. Chew slowly and savour each bite, fully experiencing the nourishment it provides.

• *Take mindful breaks*: Throughout the day, take short breaks to pause, breathe, and recenter yourself. Notice your surroundings, the sensations in your body, and any emotions or thoughts that arise.

Mindful Thinking in Relationships:

- ***Be fully present during conversations***: When engaging with others, give them your undivided attention. Listen actively, without interrupting, and respond mindfully, considering your words and their impact.

- ***Cultivate empathy***: Put yourself in others' shoes, trying to understand their perspective and emotions. Practice compassion and non-judgment, allowing for more meaningful connections.

- ***Notice and manage reactive patterns***: When conflicts arise, be aware of your emotional reactions and take a moment to respond thoughtfully rather than reacting impulsively. This can foster healthier communication and conflict resolution.

Mindful Thinking in Work or Studies:

• *Set mindful intentions*: Before starting a task, clarify your intentions and purpose. This helps you stay focused and engaged, avoiding distractions and procrastination.

• *Single-tasking over multitasking*: Instead of trying to do multiple things at once, focus on one task at a time. Give it your full attention, and once completed, move on to the next task mindfully.

• *Take mindful breaks*: Incorporate short breaks throughout your work or study sessions to rest your mind and recharge. Use this time for deep breathing, stretching, or engaging in a calming activity.

Mindful Thinking in Self-Care:

• ***Prioritize self-care activities***: Engage in activities that nourish your mind, body, and soul. Whether it's taking a walk in nature, practicing yoga, or journaling, allocate time for activities that bring you joy and relaxation.

• ***Notice and manage stress***: Pay attention to the signs of stress in your body and mind. Practice deep breathing, meditation, or progressive muscle relaxation to alleviate stress and promote relaxation.

• ***Cultivate self-compassion***: Treat yourself with kindness and understanding. When faced with challenges or setbacks, practice self-compassion by acknowledging your efforts and embracing imperfections.

Remember, integrating mindful thinking into various aspects of your life is an ongoing practice. Start by incorporating small mindful moments throughout your day and gradually expand your practice. With consistency and patience, you can develop a greater sense of mindfulness, leading to a more fulfilling and balanced life.

ABOUT THE AUTHOR
Rob Taylor

Rob Taylor is a nonfiction author dedicated to exploring truth, clarity, and the human experience. His works challenge illusions and invite readers to live with greater awareness and alignment to reality.

He is the author of The Philosophy of Veritism: Beyond Religion, Beyond Atheism, Toward Reality, a groundbreaking call to live by evidence, reason, and truth in an age of confusion. His earlier works include Mastering the Art of Mindful Thinking, a practical guide to cultivating clarity and resilience in everyday life, and The Prince of Pico, a reflective memoir capturing a transformative chapter of his life in Los Angeles during the early 2000s.

Across his writing, Taylor's aim is consistent: to empower readers with the tools to think clearly, act wisely, and live authentically.

Also by Rob Taylor:

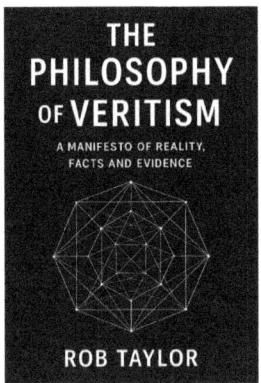

A New Philosophy for Our Time

My new book, The Philosophy of Veritism: Beyond Religion, Beyond Atheism, Toward Reality, offers a bold framework for living authentically in an age clouded by noise and division.

This isn't just theory — it's a call to clarity.

A call to live in alignment with what is real, not what is merely believed.

Step into the conversation. Step into reality.

The Prince of Pico

A memoir of transformation, creativity, and resilience.

All books available now in Ebook, paperback and hardcover

www.ingramcontent.com/pod-product-compliance
Lightning Source LLC
Chambersburg PA
CBHW040108100526
44584CB00029BA/3912